Original title:
The Unsolved Mysteries of Living

Copyright © 2025 Creative Arts Management OÜ
All rights reserved.

Author: Evelyn Hartman
ISBN HARDBACK: 978-1-80566-150-4
ISBN PAPERBACK: 978-1-80566-445-1

Mysteries woven in Twilight

In twilight's glow, the cat walks tall,
Whispers secrets only he can call.
Why do shadows dance and prance?
Are they teaching us how to romance?

A sock went missing, where could it be?
The laundry basket holds a secret spree.
Perhaps the dryer's a portal to Mars?
Or it's hiding to mend its little scars?

Unraveled Threads of Existence

Life's a ball of yarn, all tangled up,
Cats take a sip from the empty cup.
Questions bubble like soda in a glass,
Who decided that chickens are allowed to pass?

The coffee's strong, yet I feel quite weak,
Mornings are funny, with monkeys at their peak.
What if spoons are trying to run away?
They're tired of stirring, come what may!

Lost Connections in Crowded Places

In crowds we bump, yet eyes stay blind,
A parade of faces, yet none aligned.
Phone in hand but it's lost in the sea,
Did it go to Bermuda? Just like me?

Strangers flickering, like bad Wi-Fi,
Did I wave or just flail my arms in the sky?
Why does no one dance in grocery aisles?
A cart full of pure joy fuels my smiles.

The Puzzle of Fragile Moments

Moments slip through like grains of sand,
Tickle me funny, I don't understand.
Why do we listen to a clock's big tune?
When it only sings for the light of the moon?

Holding laughter like a fragile glass,
It might just shatter—oh, let it pass!
Life's a juggling act, but I'm out of balls,
Like juggling eggs and waiting for the falls!

Awkward Truths in Suave Lies

In a world where cats can rule,
We chase after dreams just like a fool.
With socks that never seem to match,
And breakfast served from a paper patch.

Mirrors lie, they stretch and twist,
Who knew a waistline could be so missed?
We take the plunge yet barely dive,
Crafting tales where only we survive.

Ciphers Hidden in Plain Sight

Coffee cups with secret codes,
Each sip a story, as the morning explodes.
Who wrote the poem on the wall?
Was it me, or just a small droolfall?

The keys to life are nowhere to find,
In sock drawers or in your mind.
Philosophers wear shoes untied,
While pigeons giggle and openly bide.

Riddles Wrapped in Silence

Why does the fridge hum late at night?
Is it dreaming of food, or gearing for flight?
The cat at the window, with her know-it-all gaze,
Knows more about life than all of our ways.

In whispers, the walls share the latest news,
About socks that vanish and rhythm-less blues.
Our laughter echoes while secrets confide,
In riddles that shimmer, without a guide.

The Geometry of Longing

Triangles form in the strangest of ways,
Like love notes folded in schoolyard plays.
The heart's a compass, but don't ask it why,
It points in all directions, often awry.

Angles of awkwardness, sharp like a knife,
Cut through the silence of everyday life.
When longing's a circle, it's endlessly round,
Smiling at dancers who trip on the ground.

Tapestry of Unanswered Questions

Why do socks vanish in the wash?
Is the dryer a portal to a land?
Where all lost things go for a nosh,
And our feet have nothing left to stand?

Do cats know secrets we can't see?
Are they plotting a coup for the throne?
With their purring conspiracies, glee,
Should we trust them when we're alone?

Why do we chase after fleeting dreams?
While reality watches and grins?
Is life more than it seems at first beams?
Or just a dance where everyone spins?

Can the fridge talk back when it hums?
Pending rumors of food going sour?
Or do it just coast on electric drums,
Counting the minutes till midnight's hour?

Lurking Beneath the Surface

They say the goldfish knows our fate,
With bubbles that spell out our plight.
But is it true or just a bait?
A fishy tale that swims through the night?

What lurks beneath the couch's edge?
Fingers crossed for more than dust bunnies.
Could it be treasure or a pledge?
Or that missing sandwich from the stories?

When clouds roll in, we often wonder,
Are they hiding secrets or lost fries?
Do they chuckle at us under thunder,
Holding weather jokes in their skies?

Is coffee just a smooth disguise,
For sleepy dreams we never own?
Each sip a riddle in disguise,
While caffeinated thoughts have grown?

The Essence of Enigmatic Journeys

Off we go, on this bumpy ride,
Maps upside down, we're on a quest.
With snacks in tow, smiles wide with pride,
Who knew adventure was such a jest?

Why do we pack so many things?
Only to use but half in the end?
Is it the thrill that packing brings,
Or just our love for the unexpected bend?

Do we ever truly find our way,
Or just hop from one whim to another?
Perhaps it's all just child's play,
With giggles hiding under the covers.

Are the roads alive or just paved?
With whispers of stories unheard?
Each bump a laugh, a memory saved,
On journeys where whimsy's preferred?

Through the Lens of Uncertainty

Why is my phone always on mute?
Yet shares my thoughts without my say?
Is it a sign or just plain brute,
A silent partner in my dismay?

When I wear my socks without a pair,
Is that fashion or simply despair?
Do shoes all laugh at my bold flair,
As I wobble in mismatched affair?

Why do we question every little thing?
While squirrels hold conferences on the lawn?
Are they plotting, or just on a swing,
As we ponder why the dawn has drawn?

With each moment, a twist to explore,
Uncertainty dances, we twirl and spin.
Is laughter the answer to wanting more?
In this riddle, let the fun begin!

Labyrinths of Dreams and Desires

In a dream, I found a shoe,
What size, I thought, could it be?
A slipper for a giant's foot,
Or perhaps just lost on a spree.

I chased a rabbit, quite absurd,
It wore a hat and spoke of tea.
"Join the party!" it had slurred,
But tripped on crumbs and then set free.

I wandered through a forest dense,
Where trees gave riddles, tall and stout.
Each answer led to more suspense,
And left me laughing, filled with doubt.

What puzzle lies in every whim?
The cat just grinned, I swear it did.
With each new turn, the lights grow dim,
But every twist just kept us hid.

The Dance of Uncertainty and Fate

I twirled with fate, a wild dance,
She stepped on toes, oh what a mess!
With every spin, I took a chance,
And traded grace for sheer excess.

A fortune teller with a grin,
Predicted soup for lunch today.
I asked her why, she shrugged my kin,
"You'll find your luck in cold puree!"

The stars above are quite confused,
They sparkled bright, then fell asleep.
They joked about the paths we choose,
And left us all with dreams to keep.

So kick your shoes, and laugh a lot,
Life's a jest, a circus show.
Embrace the tumble, tie the knot,
And dance through mysteries, with a bow.

Expressions Lost to Time

In a scrapbook filled with sunny smiles,
I found a note, quite dated too.
It said, "Beware the crocodile,"
But all I saw were eggshells blue.

An old clock ticked without a care,
It told me hours were mere fakes.
So I set off without a dare,
To find the cake that time forsakes.

With every wrinkle on my face,
There hides a story, laugh or cry.
A dance of thoughts, a silly race,
Of giggles lost that zoomed on by.

So cherish now each silly face,
As life tosses pies and quakes.
For in each laugh, a sweet embrace,
Shows time's a jester, full of breaks.

Whispers of Forgotten Memories

In dusty corners, whispers dwell,
Of things we've done, and things we've said.
There's laughter stuck in every shell,
Barefoot adventures that we led.

The time I lost my shoe in mud,
And wrestled vines with a wild grin.
Those moments fade but leave a flood,
Of echoes dancing in my skin.

A box of trinkets, filled with giggles,
Each object holds a tale untold.
From rubber bands to old lost jiggles,
They paint a life that's bright and bold.

So let us dig through layers deep,
And chase the shadows, old and spry.
For in these whims, our hearts do leap,
With whispers of the days gone by.

Together Yet Apart

We're like socks that lost their mates,
In the dryer of life's fates.
Waving hands, we stand aloof,
In our own silly groove.

Laughter echoes through the halls,
A distant friend behind the walls.
Texting memes while I sip tea,
Oh, how strange this life can be.

Juggling dreams with potato chips,
Wink from afar, no need for slips.
Moroccan rugs in virtual space,
Dancing in a ghostly place.

In our own worlds, we plot and scheme,
Each laugh an oddball, ridiculous dream.
Together yet apart, it's oh so clear,
Like two left shoes that just won't adhere.

Fragments of a Puzzle Unmade

A missing piece beneath the couch,
Turned up on my pet's bed — ouch!
A cat that thinks it's hide and seek,
With jigsaw dreams that make me squeak.

Puzzles scatter 'round my floor,
Each piece a mystery I should explore.
But half the time, I just sit back,
Counting chips from last night's snack.

Why do I need a perfect fit?
A crooked smile just makes me sit!
Fragments pieced in a crazy rhyme,
Dance like fools, we won't waste time.

So here we are, just mismatched fun,
Life's a puzzle, never done.
In a game where laughter's queen,
Fragmented joy, an endless scene.

The Color of Shadows

Shadows loiter in the noon,
Like mischievous kids with a tune.
Some dance silly; others sneak,
They tease the light; it's all so bleak.

Wearing cloaks of midnight blue,
They gossip and play hide-and-seek too.
Once they trip on a city's glow,
Spilling secrets I'd never know.

In playful hues they drape the ground,
Yet when caught, they make no sound.
Whispers of color, all aglow,
A riddle only the sun might show.

With shadows here, who needs the sun?
Living loud, oh what fun!
In every shade and every hue,
A painted life in whispered view.

Ephemeral Secrets of the Heart

Butterflies dancing, love at first sight,
Whispers that flutter, oh what a plight.
Hearts do the cha-cha, skip and sway,
In a whirlwind of dreams that lead us astray.

A tangle of wishes, a twinkle in the eye,
Cupcakes of laughter as we float by.
Our hearts write poems in the air,
While we trip on pants, unaware.

Chasing the clouds, we giggle and squeak,
Each glance a secret, each smile unique.
In fleeting moments, we make a start,
Painting the air with our heavy heart.

So let's embrace the strange parade,
In this wacky game of love unmade.
With blushing cheeks and hearts that ignite,
Ephemeral wonders, what a delight!

Constellations of Complicated Lives

In the cosmos of coffee spills,
We laugh at our daily thrills.
Mars is just a missing sock,
Venus, a lost TikTok clock.

Asteroids are just bad hair days,
While stars groove in quirky ways.
Galaxies of mismatched dreams,
Orbiting life's funny schemes.

The Weight of a Thousand Secrets

I hid a cookie in my shoe,
A secret that I thought I knew.
The weight of crumbs is so absurd,
With every step, a sparkly word.

My cat knows where they all are stashed,
She chuckles as our snacks are mashed.
Whispers of cake in the fridge,
That's a mystery, up on the ridge.

Enigmas Smiling in the Shadows

In the corner, shadows play,
Hiding giggles, come what may.
Laughter slips through cracks and seams,
As we juggle oddball dreams.

What's that noise? A phantom cat?
Or maybe just my old baseball hat?
Mysteries in every nook,
Sometimes, we forget how to look.

Unfolding Mysteries in Simple Acts

A wink from the mailman passing by,
Leaves us wondering why, oh why?
He's carrying such a weight,
Is it cookies or a fate?

A sneeze that stops all worldly cheer,
Is it a curse, or just a deer?
Every hiccup holds a key,
Unlocking hilarities, you and me.

Lanterns in the Mist

In twilight's grip, we drift and sway,
With lanterns lit, we bumble and play.
What's hidden there, in this foggy maze?
Do we seek answers or just a fun craze?

Ghosts of questions bob and weave,
Do we answer them or merely believe?
As shadows dance in playful delight,
We chuckle as truth hides from sight.

Mysterious glares from objects unseen,
Is that a cat or a quirky machine?
We laugh out loud, embracing our fears,
In the mist, odd tales fill our ears.

So let's wander on, with laughter we'll glide,
In this foggy maze, let joy be our guide.
The lanterns twinkle, a whimsical test,
Unraveling life's puzzles, with humor as the best.

The Weight of Unasked Questions

Hitchhiking thoughts on a bumpy road,
What if life's secrets wear a heavy load?
Do we whisper sweet nothings in vain,
Or laugh through the chaos, like it's all a game?

We ponder the 'why' with silly expressions,
Finding solace in wacky confessions.
Does the universe chuckle? Oh, who can say?
We shrug it off, blending humor and clay.

Curious minds chase quirks in a line,
Wait, what's that? Was it a cat or a pine?
Life's little puzzles tease with a grin,
Should we question at all, or just spin?

So grab your silliness, don't let it drown,
For laughter's the key to wear life's crown.
Each unasked question may hold a jest,
As we stroll this path, let humor invest.

Whispers Beneath the Surface

Underneath the waves, secrets collide,
What if fish chat while we bide our time?
Do they gossip about our silly swim?
Those awkward splashes and moments so grim?

The bubbles rise, they pop with delight,
As we fumble in pools, our foes in sight.
Does the ocean chuckle as we dive in?
Or is it waiting to reel us back out again?

Mermaids may laugh at our flailing feet,
As they whisper sweet tales, oh, what a treat!
We splash and we swirl with delightful flair,
Unraveling jokes in the ocean's own lair.

So let's dive deeper, with a wink and a grin,
Among the whispers where the silliness spins.
Beneath the surface where fun holds the reins,
We'll swim through life, dodging all the mundane pains.

Shadows of Forgotten Paths

In winding lanes where shadows flicker,
We stumble on mysteries, bright and snicker.
Did that tree bow, or is it just me?
Laughing at secrets of what we can't see?

Old paths may lead to places bizarre,
Full of odd trinkets and a hint of a scar.
What creatures wander these twilight scenes?
Do they ponder our jackets or peek in our jeans?

A ticklish breeze makes the night feel bold,
As shadows engage in stories retold.
Are they laughing at us, or are we all game?
In these forgotten paths, it's all the same.

So embrace the odd, in quirks we invest,
Create tales of laughter, let silliness nest.
For every shadow carries a whimsical light,
As we roam forgotten paths, full of delight.

Echoes of Untold Stories

In the closet, old shoes dance,
Forgotten tales, not a chance.
A sock with a hole claims it can sing,
While dust bunnies cheer, 'Let's do our thing!'

The cat believes she's a sleek spy,
Stalking the curtains, oh my, oh my!
Unraveling secrets of the old rug,
With a flick of her tail, she gives it a shrug.

The fridge hums wearied, a tired bard,
Its leftovers gathered, playing cards.
A slice of lasagna whispers a joke,
While ketchup bottles plot, 'Let's make a smoke!'

In the bathroom, the soap has a plan,
To slip on the floor and laugh like a man.
With each splash and foam, a giggle ignites,
As bubbles escape into whimsical flights.

Secrets in the Dance of Time

Tick-tock on the wall with a grin,
Winking at moments that bubble within.
Clocks play hide-and-seek with no end,
As seconds pirouette, trying to blend.

The toaster's a DJ poppin' bread jams,
While toast goes wild, breaking all plans.
"Too hot to handle!" it announces with glee,
With breakfast beats that are funky and free.

Note pads conspire on who to tell,
About the laundry that danced quite well.
Clothes flapped their sleeves in a wild spun spree,
"Pick me! No, pick me!" they shouted with glee.

Calendars fold and unfold into shapes,
As Tuesday's dressed up in silly capes.
With a wink and a nudge, they laugh through the days,
In a swirl of confusion, a merry delay.

Unwritten Pages of Existence

Pages blank, but the pens have a dream,
To scribble odd tales that burst at the seam.
With doodles of dragons and cats wearing hats,
And fish that ride bikes, oh where are the bats?

The chair in the corner has gossip to share,
About shadows that jump and dance without care.
With cushions all chuckling at secrets untold,
As they prank the old table that looks really old.

In the fridge, ancient sauces swap stories,
Of life as a condiment, full of glories.
Mustard jumps in with a sneeze so loud,
While ketchup plays coy, "I'm too cool for the crowd!"

Books on the shelf roll their eyes with a sigh,
Lamenting the plots that forgot how to fly.
Invisible ink fades into the space,
As characters wait for a wild, silly chase.

Chasing Shadows in Daylight

Sunbeams chase dust like a game of tag,
While shadows slip by in a stealthy zigzag.
The sofa sighs softly, a cloud of repose,
As it dreams of wild adventures, who knows?

Bicycles lean with stories to tell,
Of rides through the park and that time they fell.
With training wheels squeaking a wobbly tune,
While squirrels raise their glasses, "To the great noon!"

Trees tell of whispers in rustling leaves,
Barking at clouds that wear silly sleeves.
With every gust, the branches will sway,
And laughter tumbles down in a playful spray.

In corners of sunlight, the ants form a line,
Marching to the rhythm of summertime pine.
"Join us!" they chant, in a chorus so sweet,
Even the shadows can't help but tap their feet.

The Play of Light and Dark

In a world of shadows where the giggles creep,
The sun plays hide-and-seek, a game so deep.
A cat jumps high, a shadowy blur,
While dogs fetch dreams, caught in a purr.

The moon winks bright, a silver joke,
As crickets chirp, an evening cloak.
We dance in circles, oh what a sight,
Underneath the stars, laughter takes flight.

The trees whisper secrets, a rustling cheer,
While squirrels debate which nut to share.
Time ticks funny, like a clown's old watch,
In this world of riddles, do we ever catch?

So let's paint our lives with shades of glee,
And tickle the ribs of the mystery spree.
For every puzzle holds a giggling spark,
In the light and dark, we leave our mark.

Questions Carried by the Wind

Why does the toaster always burn my bread?
Is it planning a prank, in its metal head?
The breeze asks the trees, why dance so wide?
While flowers giggle at bees, buzzing with pride.

What if the clouds have a soft, fluffy plan?
To rain down confetti while they can?
The sun shouts questions, in rays that flick,
As shadows reply with a playful flick.

Can time take a break, and share a good laugh?
Or is it too busy drawing life's path?
The squirrels have answers, all wrapped in their fluff,
But only if you can keep up with their stuff.

So as questions float on a breeze of delight,
Let's weigh them with smiles, in day and in night.
For living's a dance, a whimsical jest,
A quirk of existence, we'll never outguess.

Chasing the Elusive Dawn

Rising early, fog in my hair,
Coffee brews, no sign of a bear.
Chasing sunlight, tripping on lace,
What's out there? A curious face!

Birds sing songs, I hum along,
Is that a tune or a crow's strong?
What's the rush to greet the sun?
Maybe it just wants to run!

Chasing shadows, skipping on grass,
I fall down, what a classy pass!
Snickerdoodle skaters on ice,
I guess the dawn thinks it's nice!

So I'll keep dancing, laugh and twirl,
Maybe tomorrow, I'll catch that swirl!
Gone before lunch, like a quick balloon,
Dawn giggles softly, see you soon!

Portraits of Fleeting Moments

Captured smiles, with ice cream drips,
Moments freeze, on sugar lips.
A wink, a laugh, a fleeting glance,
Who knew life was such a dance?

Snap a shot, the dog steals fries,
Chasing squirrels, we hear their cries.
Neighborhood gossip, a tangled yarn,
What is real, a cat in a barn?

At the fair, a balloon flies high,
I reach for dreams, they wave goodbye.
Fortunes told by a clown so wise,
Is the joke on me? What a surprise!

Tick-tock goes the clock's parade,
Worry not, for laughter's made.
Each brighter pic, a tale we weave,
Moments pass, but we do believe!

Paradoxes of the Human Soul

Happiness hides behind a frown,
Jester in a golden gown.
Fragile hearts break like a glow,
Why is love also the woe?

We seek answers wrapped in jest,
Finding comfort in the rest.
Silly dreams, a wild breeze,
Who knew pondering could tease?

Two left feet on a dance floor,
I whirl and twirl, then hit the door!
Life's a riddle dressed in lace,
Giggling souls in a life race.

So grab a smile, wear it proud,
Join the chaos, join the crowd!
Paradoxes make us whole,
So let's embrace this playful role!

Shrouded in Wonder

Why do socks vanish, tell me why?
One in the dryer, the other a lie!
Hats on squirrels, they don't play fair,
What do they know that I don't dare?

Clouds whisper secrets to the moon,
While I munch on pizza, send a tune.
Floating wishes on a star,
Maybe I'm dreaming, or travel far!

Unruly thoughts swirling like ice,
Do fish have feelings, or think twice?
With every giggle, joyfully blunder,
Life's just a dance, shrouded in wonder!

So grab a lemon, make it sweet,
Life's a feast, can't be beat!
Under the sky, we find our place,
Oh, what a whimsical race!

A Dance with the Unseen

In shadows we twirl, a jolly crew,
With winks at the moon, and giggles, too.
Invisible partners lead us around,
In the silent waltz, where laughter's the sound.

Our feet tap the ground, but ghosts take the lead,
We stumble and trip, on laughter we feed.
Watch out for the cat, it leaps in the air,
A dance with the unseen, a delightful affair.

Each step is a riddle, a whisper, a jest,
In this quirky ballroom, we're all a bit blessed.
So twirl with your specters, embrace the unknown,
For in this lighthearted dance, we're never alone.

So do we take chances, or sip on the tea?
In this grand masquerade, just let yourself be.
With a chuckle and grin, we jaunt through the night,
In the dance of the unseen, our hearts take flight.

Veils of Perception

Behind every curtain, a funny surprise,
Peeking through windows, it winks at our eyes.
Reality bends like a noodle in broth,
What's true and what's fiction? Just toss out the cloth.

With glasses askew, the world looks so bright,
A rainbow of nonsense, a whimsical sight.
We ponder our fate with a giggle and sigh,
As we chase down the truth with a pie in the sky.

We juggle our dreams like a clown at a fair,
As our thoughts drift away like the fragrance of air.
Veiled in confusion, we dance and we play,
For laughter's the compass that shows us the way.

So let out a chuckle when logic stands still,
In the maze of perception, it's laughter we fill.
With smiles on our faces, we tiptoe along,
In a world full of quirks, our hearts sing the song.

The Art of Living in Between

Caught in the midst of a whimsical mess,
We juggle our dreams, with no need to impress.
In between the chaos, there's coffee and cheer,
Where the moments are muddled, but crystal clear.

With socks on our hands and hats on our feet,
We stride through this life on a dance that's elite.
Navigating conundrums with laughter as glue,
We find the absurd is what carries us through.

From the mundane to magic, we flip and we flop,
In the spaces of in-between, we giggle and hop.
With a wink at the stars, and a nod to the sun,
Living in balance is actually fun!

So embrace every pause, give a chuckle, a grin,
For the art of existing is where we all win.
In the in-betweens, life's a delightful tease,
So laugh with abandon, do just as you please.

The Ghosts We Carry

We're haunted by smiles of those we once knew,
Their laughter still lingers like morning dew.
With each step we take, they dance at our side,
In this playful parade, they swell with our pride.

From hiccups of memories that tickle our hearts,
To echoes of laughter, where nostalgia starts.
These ghosts give us courage to leap and to laugh,
In the comedy show of our quirky life path.

Dressed in the costumes of days gone by,
They join in our antics, they soar and they fly.
With shenanigans shared, they whisper our name,
In this kooky ensemble, we're all a bit fame.

So raise up a toast to the spirits we share,
To the laughter that fills the sweet autumn air.
For in fog and in folly, they lighten our way,
In the fun of existence, they forever will stay.

The Invisible Thread of Destiny

In a world where ducks wear hats,
And socks mysteriously lose their mates,
I tripped on fate while munching snacks,
  Is this the twist that destiny creates?

I asked a goldfish where to go,
Yet all it did was swim in loops,
With breadcrumbs and quirky shows,
  Life's a circus run by silly troops.

Chasing my dreams on a unicycle,
Falling off as I reach for the stars,
Who knew ambition came with a cycle?
And road rash adds to character scars!

Perhaps I'm tangled in cosmic yarn,
Knitting my fate one haphazard stitch,
Laughing at life's whimsical charm,
While pondering if cake has a glitch!

Unfathomable Waters of Tomorrow

Tomorrow's waves crash with cheer,
Belly flops while I ponder the deep,
Why did I think I'd steer,
When I can't even manage my sleep?

A fish in a tie offers a deal,
"Stay afloat! The water's great!"
With a wink and a spin of the wheel,
I ponder if swimming's my fate.

The clouds above seem to giggle,
As I wobble on board my ship,
Each wave comes with a wiggle,
And coffee spills add to my trip.

Lost in a sea of unanswered fun,
Mudskippers dance in the splash,
Diving deep is how we run,
Through waters of uncertainty, I dash!

Secrets Written in the Sky

The clouds up high write notes in fluff,
But my kite got caught, how tough!
It reads like a mystery novel,
With plot twists that make me grovel.

Birds gossip about string theory,
Chirping songs of quantum plight,
Was that a wink or just a query?
I'm left guessing day and night.

I painted my hopes in sunset hues,
Only to find they mixed with frowns,
Is that a blessing or just bad news?
My canvas shifts like merry clowns.

Stargazing leads to more questions,
Like why do planets wear such bling?
DIY UFO construction sessions,
Make me wonder if they'd join my swing!

The Curiosity of Unanswered Questions

Why do cats think they own the house?
Does cheese really age like fine wine?
Each query makes me laugh, no doubt,
As I ponder the meaning of time.

What if spaghetti could tell stories?
It would twist and twirl in delight,
Recounting tales of all its glories
Under the disco ball, oh what a sight!

Is a toaster an artist or tool?
Burnt offerings served with a grin,
Or should I take a trip to a school?
To learn why it offers, but doesn't win!

Life's a parade of curious sights,
With questions dancing, never still,
Let's toast to the odd and goofy nights,
And to answers that marry with thrill!

Enigmatic Echoes of Laughter

In a world where socks disappear,
We chase the tales of whispered cheer.
Why do we laugh when we slip and fall?
Is gravity playing a game for us all?

A cat on a roof, what's he thinking?
Does he ponder while the stars are blinking?
We ponder our lives over cups of tea,
Yet why does the toast always land with glee?

Oh, the jester's cap spins with delight,
As balloons float high in a feathery flight.
Cucumbers in hats dance in the breeze,
Bringing giggles like whispers from trees.

So here we stand, tickled by fate,
Spinning tales without a straight gate.
For laughter's the riddle, the cosmic jest,
In this funny world, who needs a quest?

The Weight of Unspoken Words

Every pause carries heavy loads,
Like laundry piled up in crooked codes.
In silence we search for things to say,
But the cat still won't give up its play.

A bluebird sings of secrets untold,
While the mailbox waits for letters bold.
Why do we whisper when we could yell?
Is it fear of the neighbor's ringing bell?

Our thoughts become ballets on toes,
Yet, sometimes they trip on their own woes.
The tongue can tango, twist, and whine,
Leaving breadcrumbs on this life's fine line.

We gather our words like autumn leaves,
Crafting confessions amidst subtle thieves.
In laughter, we learn what we cannot speak,
As giggles hide truths and answers we seek.

Labyrinths of Thought and Time

A mind as messy as spaghetti strands,
Twists and turns like a circus of bands.
We question our shoes, why one's a clown,
While socks debate who's the king of the town.

Tick-tock shouts the clock from its stand,
Yet hours wander off like grains of sand.
"Why is it Monday?" we sigh with dread,
As time sneaks away like a cat that is fed.

Thoughts bouncing 'round like rubber balls,
We chase the echoes down endless halls.
A sheep in a dream tries to count us instead,
But we're too busy wondering where socks have fled.

In this maze, we trip, we giggle, we fall,
Finding joy in the chaos that shapes us all.
For in the labyrinths of our own tricky mind,
The humor we stumble upon is one of a kind.

Veils of Perception

Behind each curtain, a clown might hide,
With pies and giggles, he'll turn the tide.
We squint at the world through tinted glass,
While pondering deep, which marbles to class.

A mirror may lie, but reflections can tease,
As we skip through puddles, giggling with ease.
Why do we trip over bricks that are words?
Perhaps life's a dance with invisible birds.

The veil may shimmer, a shroud of delight,
Revealing the wonders of day into night.
Look close at the fog, see the truth beneath,
Where laughter can bloom like a joyful wreath.

For our perceptions twist like a winding road,
Carrying us forth with laughter as code.
With each silly lens we decide to behold,
The world becomes brighter, and never grows old.

Fragments of a Hidden Truth

In a world of sock-less feet,
You look for pairs that run on repeat.
They vanish into unseen nooks,
Leaving you with all the crannies and crooks.

The cat eyes the fridge with a stance,
As if it knows there's a secret dance.
You scratch your head, try to deduce,
But it just purrs, giving you no truce.

Why does my phone ring with no one there?
Is it the ghost of voicemail's despair?
I answer, hoping for a sweet tune,
Instead, it's just silence, a cosmic cartoon.

In dreams, I fly, but always fall,
Maybe it's truth doing a pratfall.
I wake up grinning, scratching my head,
Was it a farce? Or something I said?

Chronicles of the Unknowable

Once I tried to bake a pie,
But the recipe was a sly goodbye.
Flour clouds, a whisk gone rogue,
Now I'm left with a pudding fog.

Found a sock in the toaster's glow,
Was that a prank from my cat or faux?
She smirks, tapping her whiskered chin,
I'm left to ponder, where to begin?

The neighbor says there's a ghost in the wall,
But it just plays jokes: a very loud call.
It sneezes my name in the dead of night,
I can't help but giggle, it's a comical fright.

Why do we laugh when things go awry?
Maybe life's just a continuous pie sky.
Keep rolling the dough, let it breathe,
Each mishap a treasure, in chaos we weave.

Reflections from the Abyss

I stared at my rent document, aghast,
In this financial game, am I outclassed?
I checked my bank, only crickets chirped,
Is that a sign or have I just burped?

I tried jogging, but ran on the spot,
An ultra-relaxed version of a thought.
I tripped on my laces, danced with the breeze,
Who knew flailing was a professional tease?

The dog in the park shakes hands with fate,
While all I can do is contemplate.
Maybe it's better to fetch your own ball,
With laughter aplenty, we might still stand tall.

Fish in a pond plot their great escape,
While I wonder how to reshape my fate.
Who knew the abyss had such a fun line?
In deep contemplation, I'm sipping on brine.

The Nature of Unfinished Stories

A sandwich half-made sits on the plate,
Does it feel abandoned or just late?
Peanut butter dreams and jelly tears,
Waiting for someone to connect the gears.

In the library, books whisper in code,
What if they've all just gone rogue?
They shuffle their pages, a sly little wink,
If they could talk, oh, what would they think?

A puzzle with pieces hidden away,
Do they giggle at our effort to play?
One corner's upside down, causing a fuss,
Yet in chaos, I find a curious plus.

So I dance with uncertainty, a clumsy affair,
Does a twist in the road lead us somewhere?
In the book of life, maybe there's more,
Than just closing chapters, but an open door.

Secrets Beneath the Surface

Why do socks vanish in the wash?
Maybe they fly off for a big ol' posh.
With parties for lint and threads galore,
They dance in circles, who could ask for more?

Coffee cups seem to hide and flee,
Are they plotting with the cutlery?
Spoons whisper secrets, in hushed tones they rhyme,
While plates giggle softly, lost in their prime.

The cat looks wise, like it knows the score,
Is it planning a coup? I'm not too sure.
I feed it fish and it gives me a stare,
Perhaps it's the ruler of this empire's lair.

At night the fridge hums a tropical tune,
Is it aware of the snackers' monsoon?
Each shelf holds treasures, might be a trap,
Is it dessert heaven, or just a catnap?

Threads of Unseen Connection

My phone drops calls like it's in a game,
It giggles out loud, 'Ain't that a shame?'
And yet, my neighbor's voice rings crystal clear,
Is my phone dating them? I sense something queer.

Traffic lights blink like they lost a bet,
Waiting so long, we all start to sweat.
Do they have secrets in the color of red?
Perhaps they are plotting the next big spread.

The weather forecast is often a spout,
Is it just fun to leave folks in doubt?
Parachuting raindrops on sunny bright days,
Soaking us down while the sunlight just plays.

I drop my keys, they sprout wings and fly,
'Catch me if you can!' they cheekily cry.
Do they have dreams of soaring the skies?
Or just seeking freedom from mundane ties?

Enigmas of the Everyday

Why does my toast always land on the floor?
With a flip and a flutter, it yearns to explore.
Is it staging a coup with the jam and the bread?
Perhaps they're plotting to join the spread?

Mirrors reflect who we wish to be,
But do they giggle at our clumsy spree?
They hold our secrets, with glimmers of truth,
And laugh when we pretend to reclaim our youth.

A chair creaks loud like it's gossiping,
Has it caught wind of my nesting fling?
Every squeak feels like it's in on the joke,
While I trip over words and their playful poke.

Mystery soup in the fridge, what's the plan?
Is it a potion or just something bland?
Each sip is an adventure, a wild surprise,
Maybe it knows the secret of the skies?

Illusions of Certainty

Calendars pass like they're in a race,
Each day a canvas, we scribble our grace.
Yet the hours slip by just as quick as a wink,
Turns out, time is just a big cosmic prank.

Maps claim to guide us, but oh what a thrill,
They twist and they turn when I look for a chill.
Are they teasing me while I'm lost in a maze?
Or planning a party for the lost in a daze?

Shoes steer you wrong, and they sneakily play,
One moment I'm right, next I'm whisked away.
Are my toes protesting or just planning a strike?
One step leads to laughter, another to hike.

The clock takes its chances with ticks and tocks,
Collecting our moments like rare little rocks.
When certainty winks, and chaos takes root,
We dance through the riddles in life's funny suit.

Echoes of Lives Not Lived

If I were a cat, what could I dream?
A life full of naps and a diet of cream.
But here I am, sipping my tea,
Wondering if cats ever ponder on me.

In parallel worlds, I speak fluent whale,
I waltz with the wind and I dance with the sail.
Yet back in my chair, I chuckle and sigh,
Imagining fish in a tuxedo tie.

Sometimes I'm royal, adorned with a crown,
Others I'm a jester, just clowning around.
With each silly thought, I can't help but grin,
Oh, what a fun place this life I've been in!

So raise a glass to the lives we might chase,
To dreams and to giggles that time can't erase.
In the laughter of echoes, we all overlap,
Mysteries wrapped in a whimsical wrap.

The Camouflage of Differences

We're all in this game, dressed up like spies,
Wearing fancy masks and silly disguise.
From rich pastries layered with icing,
To plain old cheese, everyone's enticing.

We dance to the beat of a strange little tune,
Beneath disco balls, underneath a cartoon.
A robot with rhythm, or a plant in a hat,
Changing the world in a chatty sprawl that's flat.

With quirks like a jazz band and giggles galore,
We find a strange harmony—who could ask for more?
In oversized shoes and two different socks,
We march to the beat of our paradox clocks.

So celebrate oddities and what makes us bright,
Mix paint with your laughter—let's paint it delight!
For in every oddball, a spark of truth shines,
In this fun little carnival where each one defines.

Dreams in the Attic of Time

In the attic, I found a relic of dreams,
A kazoo that sings, and rickety beams.
Old laughter trapped in a dusty old chest,
And wishes that danced in their fanciest dress.

A paper airplane flies, the sky is its stage,
Flying past worries and flipping the page.
How many moments have come and have gone,
Clad in pajamas, from dusk until dawn?

Somehow, I'm an astronaut, soaring through space,
Riding on comets with sparkles to chase.
These dreams whisper softly, tickling my mind,
In time's cozy attic, wonder's well-defined.

Yet time's sneaky grip can make laughter fade,
So I crank up the kazoo and let memories parade!
For dreams wrapped in giggles can never grow old,
In the attic of hearts, their magic unfolds.

Dualities Amidst Harmony

I'm the early bird, but I sleep 'til noon,
A night owl, too, under the glow of the moon.
In this duality, I sing out of tune,
Chasing my dreams with a bright plastic spoon.

Beneath the clamor of the world's busy cheer,
Lies the peace of a nap, tucked in with a deer.
One foot in chaos, the other in grace,
Juggling my socks in this wild, joyful race.

I'm a sandwich in traffic, a dance on the line,
An enigma that's just a well-seasoned twine.
With every twist and turn of our fates,
Life cooks us up with odd, tasty plates.

So let's toast to the plays of our curious roles,
And laugh through the twists that life gently tolls.
In this recipe of fun, we might just find bliss,
Dualities dance in a world not amiss.

Forgotten Names in the Sand

A name etched in the grain, it fades,
Like ice cream on a sunny day,
Was it Bob, or maybe Sue?
Now I'm lost, what do I say?

Each wave that rolls just washes it out,
Like secrets that we try to keep,
Was that a wink or just a pout?
Oh, the laughter makes us leap!

I found a shell, it whispered 'Jay',
But is that really true?
Or just a trick of the seaside play?
I guess I'll never have a clue!

So I'll write my name then walk away,
Maybe this time it will remain,
But with each tide, I'll surely sway,
Another quest in the sand's domain!

Intrigues of a Starry Night

Under the stars, I lost my shoe,
Was it the moon that stole the light?
Or did I trip on something blue?
Ah, the mysteries of the night!

Constellations whisper tales so grand,
Of aliens and things unseen,
But who would take my other hand?
A riddle wrapped in silver sheen.

The owls hoot secrets, wise and sage,
What stories do they truly fake?
Is my blanket just a cosmic page?
Or is that UFO a big mistake?

With every shooting star, I grin,
Do wishes count as footnotes too?
The laughter dances, all within,
In this wacky cosmic view!

The Language of Shadows

Shadows dance with giggles at noon,
Are they plotting with the light?
With every shift, I hear a tune,
Whispers of mischief slight.

A shadow hides, and then it creaks,
Is that my hat, or a hat in disguise?
It sneaks and slips, so sly it sneaks,
Reflecting my own surprise!

With every flicker, the game is on,
Are they my pals or outlaws bold?
When light pulls back, they're drawn upon,
A mystery subtle, a tale retold.

So I'll laugh with shadows, each one a friend,
They'll tell me tales, 'til the light shall bend,
In their company, the fun won't end,
For laughter weaves, a humor to lend!

Riddles in the Rain

Puddles crunch beneath my feet,
Do raindrops laugh or just float down?
They splatter stories, oh so sweet,
In the city or the town.

Clouds debate on what to wear,
Is that a coat or just a cloak?
With every drip, I lose my flair,
Rain's riddle grows as I provoke!

Umbrellas flip, a sail gone wrong,
I leap and dodge like a silly fish,
But laughter bursts, a joyful song,
Who's to say what we really wish?

So dance through rain, embrace the mess,
For every drop is just a jest,
A playful splash, no need to stress,
In riddles told, we find our best!

Threads of Fate Yet Untangled

A cat crossed my path, oh what a scare,
But really, it's just fluff, without a care.
Like losing socks in the laundry spree,
Could fate be tangled yarn, or just a tree?

Each twist and turn has its own little joke,
Like mixing up coffee with hot diet coke.
We laugh and we stumble on this grand parade,
A dance with the awkward, a laugh at the fade.

Sometimes I ponder the paths we all take,
As I trip on my shoelace, oh what a mistake!
Yet in this great chaos, there's joy to be found,
Like confetti at parties that rain from the ground.

So here's to the knots and the laughs that we share,
To fates intertwined—like spaghetti in air.
Let's weave in our quirks, our moments of glee,
For life's just a thread, we can twirl, you and me.

The Sound of Silence in Motion

I tried to hear silence, turned up the spree,
But all that I caught was a buzz from the bee.
Like echoes of laughter in a quiet café,
Where whispers of secrets are thrown on display.

In moments of stillness, the chaos can reign,
Like socks in the wash that just can't entertain.
I giggle at whispers that dance in my ears,
As a snail's serenade chases away all my fears.

It's funny how silence can sometimes be loud,
Like a cat purring softly, yet feeling so proud.
Each rustle and murmur, a comedy show,
As I slip on a banana peel, whoa—oh no!

So let's embrace silence, a quirk of our lives,
A hint of the silly where true laughter thrives.
In the sound of stillness, let's wiggle and sway,
For life's just a dance; let's join in the play!

Fleeting Moments, Endless Questions

A wink from a stranger, what does it imply?
Is it fortune or just a flirty goodbye?
Each moment in time is a puzzle to piece,
Like socks that play hide and seek for release.

Life's questions are like clouds, they float and they drift,
Why's toast always landing butter side adrift?
We ponder the cosmos and the why's and the how's,
While searching for meaning in the oddest of vows.

Yet even as time slips through fingers like sand,
Laughing at moments, it all becomes grand.
The tickle of time may rush us along,
But giggles and joy make our hearts feel so strong.

So join in the dance of the quickness we chase,
Let questions be laughter, let's quicken our pace.
For fleeting moments come wrapped in a jest,
To remind us of life's wild and wonderful quest!

Ghosts in the Garden of Dreams

In the garden of dreams, strange specters reside,
Dressed up in petunias, they dance and they glide.
Whispering secrets of what might have been,
While carrots in costumes smile with a grin.

With riddles they toss, like seeds in the air,
"Why do we water when we just want a chair?"
The ghosts giggle softly, like leaves in the breeze,
Turning weeds into wishes with grace and with ease.

Each flower has tales of the day's silly chase,
As daisies tell stories of losing the race.
While haunted by laughter, we wander aligned,
In the garden of whimsies, our hearts intertwined.

So come stroll with phantoms beneath starlit skies,
Where roses tell jokes, and the daisies tell lies.
Together we'll dance with the echoes of schemes,
In this wild paradise of gardens and dreams!

Searching for Clues in Moonlight

Beneath the moon's bright glow, we creep,
Chasing shadows that never sleep.
A sock misplaced, a vanished shoe,
Is it my cat or ghosts that brew?

I found a trail of glittering stars,
Wound up thinking about chocolate bars.
Whispers echo in the dark,
As my flashlight dies—oh, what a lark!

The crickets laugh, the owls hoot,
I stumble on a garden boot.
Was it left by me, or some old soul?
In mystery, there's always a hole!

So in this dance of night and whim,
I'll chase my thoughts on a moonlit swim.
Each shadow hides a silly clue,
Like finding out my fridge is askew!

Questions Lurking in the Breeze

What's that rustle in the trees?
A squirrel or the neighbor? Please!
I ponder life with each small gust,
Wondering if my plants are robust.

Are flowers gossiping 'neath the sun?
Is the grass ticklish? Could it run?
I debate with ants on who's in charge,
While seagulls squawk, feeling large.

Do clouds play tricks, or are they wise?
Spilling secrets from the skies?
A tumbleweed rolls, what does it know?
Or is it just looking for a show?

In the whispers of the breeze, I find,
A world that tickles the curious mind.
As questions dance and laughter swells,
In nature's folly, who really tells?

Hidden Patterns of a Fleeting Life

Patterns form on coffee cups,
While I mix my sugar up.
Is that a face or just a swirl?
The mess, it dances—life's a whirl!

Pasta shapes may hold a clue,
To mysteries of what I'll chew.
Are they spaghetti or just art?
Is dinner done or did it part?

I spot trends in odd socks,
Mismatched colors, ticking clocks.
Could laundry tell stories profound,
Or just be left in heaps around?

Through silly patterns, I do roam,
In the chaos, I find my home.
Each hidden thread weaves a jest,
In life's play, I'm hardly stressed!

Tides of Uncertainty

The waves crash in, then retreat,
What's left behind? A bit of cheat!
A flip-flop here, a half-eaten fry,
What's in the sea? Just don't ask why!

Sand castles sink, a royal mess,
Was it Neptune's doing? I must confess.
A crab scuttles past, with secret lore,
Or maybe it's just my beach left to explore.

Are seagulls plotting some grand affair,
While stealing fries with a swaggered glare?
With each wave, I ride my doubt,
The ocean giggles, there's no way out!

In every ebb, there's a grin concealed,
As life's silly dance is revealed.
So I float on my inflatable longe,
In tides of laughter, I'll always plunge!

Paradoxes of the Everyday

I lost my keys, but I found my mind,
While coffee spills make thoughts unwind.
My socks are odd, but my shoes are neat,
Life's funny puzzles beneath my feet.

Cats who chase, never catch a thing,
Yet grace the world like a soaring king.
A fridge that hums, but never sings,
How can chaos have such lovely wings?

The toast that lands butter-side down,
Makes mornings feel like a circus clown.
Yet in its fall, there lies a cheer,
Life's clumsy dance is what we hold dear.

In every paradox, a comic thread,
Leaves us laughing 'til we're ready for bed.
The quirks we live, the smiles we weave,
In these simple puzzles, it's joy we achieve.

Reflections in a Broken Mirror

In shards of glass, my face is split,
A jester's grin, a clown's perfect fit.
Each crack reveals a different view,
Who knew I'd need a puzzle to get through?

Laughter echoes from a frowning face,
Dancing shadows in a mishap's grace.
My hair's a nest for a bird or two,
Yet my life's a show that needs a crew.

Eyes that twinkle like shattered dreams,
Reflections twist in light's funny beams.
Mirror, mirror, what do you see?
A candid snapshot of the real me.

Embrace the flaws that make us whole,
In the laughter lies the secret role.
Each jagged edge, a quirky muse,
We wear our stories, and they amuse.

The Enigma of Heartbeats

My heart it skips, a funny dance,
Not on a date, but in a trance.
With every thump, a secret thought,
What perils lie in love's tangled knot?

Is it the chocolate or the spark?
Late-night snacks or midnight lark?
Each heartbeat's like a stand-up show,
Punchlines waiting for the right flow.

In love's embrace, the heart can race,
Yet also pause to find its place.
A riddle found in a gentle touch,
Why do we feel so much, oh so much?

So here's to pulses, wild and free,
An orchestra of joy, a symphony.
In every beat, a comical thrill,
Life's rhythm plays; let's dance at will.

Footsteps on Unmarked Roads

I wander paths that twist and bend,
Each corner turned, a funny friend.
With every step, a chuckle blooms,
As nature plays its silly tunes.

A sign that says 'This Way and That',
I walk in circles, imagine that!
The trees gossip in silent code,
In this confusion, I feel less alone.

I trip on roots, but rise with glee,
Each stumble shows the joy in me.
On roads unmarked, my joy resides,
In scenic routes of funny slides.

So follow me, if you dare to roam,
In laughter's arms, we'll find our home.
Each step we take, a giggle to share,
In life's little quirks, there's love everywhere.

Footprints in the Fog

In a mist, I step in puddles,
Each splash a silly riddle.
Who left these prints? Not me, I swear,
Maybe the cat, or that ghost over there!

Wandering through the haze, I grin,
Was that a ghost? Or just Ben's chin?
Late-night snacks? Maybe pizza's the key,
To chase away fog, just let it be!

The footprints dance, they swirl and sway,
I follow them, in a silly ballet.
But alas, they vanish, without a trace,
Leaving me with a smile on my face!

So if you find me in misty night,
Just know I'm chasing laughter, out of sight.
With each silly step, I sing a tune,
Footprints in the fog, a whimsical boon!

The Uncharted Paths of Existence

On roads unseen, I take a stroll,
With candy bags to lighten my soul.
Was that a squirrel? Or a dancing mime?
Oh wait, it's just me, losing track of time.

The grass is green, but what's that smell?
A mystery beast? Or just an old bell?
In the park, I trip on my fate,
An old shoe left by my mate.

Lost in thought, where will I be?
Maybe in a fridge, counting the peas.
An adventure awaits, if I just steer,
Away from that big scary deer!

So here's to days under the sun,
With laughter and joy, oh what fun!
Let's wander paths where none have tread,
With snacks in hand, we'll follow the bread!

Riddles of the Flickering Flame

A candle glows, it winks a plea,
What's its secret? Just let it be!
Does it know it's shorter each tick?
Maybe it's scared by the clock's loud tick.

With shadows dancing on the wall,
I swear I saw my socks take a fall.
The flame flickers with a playful grin,
I toss a marshmallow, let the fun begin.

Burnt edges, oh what a delectable sight,
Is it a treat or an edible fright?
As smoke curls up, it tickles my nose,
Just a riddle, a funny one, who knows?

So light a flame, let laughter rise,
In the warmth of jokes, we see through the lies.
With each spark, we share a beam,
Life's riddles are fun, just join the dream!

Murmurs of the Untold

In whispers soft, the stories float,
Like a pizza slice on a small goat.
What secrets linger in the night?
Probably just cats, looking for a bite.

Old trees creak with tales of yore,
Did they see me trip? Oh, what a score!
They chuckle low, I blush with glee,
Their wisdom's hidden, from you and me.

The wind's soft laugh stirs my hair,
It tells me more, but do I care?
With laughter ringing high like a bell,
I chase these murmurs, oh what the hell!

So gather 'round, dear friends, let's sing,
Of funny things that laughter will bring.
In whispers dark and truths so bright,
We find the humor in the cosmic fight!

Time's Elusive Embrace

Tick-tock goes the clock, so sly,
Just when you think you've got it, oh my!
You pour your coffee, it spills in a glee,
And time laughs, 'Catch me if you can, whee!'

The years slip by like butter on toast,
You search for your glasses, but they're on your nose!
Wrinkles appear like magic balloon art,
And you can't remember where you parked your heart.

With every birthday cake that's too sweet,
You munch on candles, a delightful treat.
Life's comedy show, with one-liners galore,
For every question, there's just more encore!

So here's to the chaos, the thrill, and the laughs,
Embracing the nonsense, in its many drafts.
In the quirky parade of the fleeting days,
We dance to the rhythm in the silliest ways.

Beneath the Surface of Ordinary Lives

In the daily grind, there's a hidden surprise,
Like finding a cat in a suit and tie!
The neighbor's dog thinks he owns the street,
While cats plot world domination in the heat.

Eggs in the morning, they often will crack,
Just like our plans, they seldom get back.
We chase after dreams with a whimsical flair,
Only to find they were hiding right there!

Each colorful sock in a drawer brings a cheer,
They plot and they scheme, but you'll never see clear.
Jellybeans dance when no one's awake,
In the mischief of life, can't afford a mistake!

So let's toast to the quirks that make life a ride,
From sneezes to giggles, let joy be our guide.
In the heart of the mundane, the silly will thrive,
Where laughter is king, and we're all more alive.

Voices from the Edge of Silence

In quiet corners, whispers prance,
Like socks that giggle, oh what a dance!
The fridge hums a tune, it's quite the croon,
While dust bunnies plot to take over the room.

A quiet sigh from the chairs, they complain,
"Does it always have to be this mundane?"
Pots gossip at night, and pans look quite sly,
As forks start a coup that leaves spoons awry.

Listen closely, the curtains will spill,
A tale of a ghost who can't pay the bill!
With every creak and moan, there's a chuckle or two,
Even the clock chimes in with some glee, who knew?

So hush your doubts and lend me your ear,
For the world sings a song that's absurd but clear.
Every faint echo holds a laugh and surprise,
In the silence, adventure is wearing disguise.

The Language of the Unseen

The dust motes dance like they own the room,
While furniture prattles in a whimsical bloom.
Light spills its secrets in sparkling delight,
As shadows debate if they're wrong or just right.

A sock's journey from washer to beach,
Maybe a vacation? The stories they teach!
Roots know the gossip of passing rain,
While leaves plot a travel against the mundane.

Under the surface, where oddities sneak,
Life's little jokes in tongues we can't speak.
Sunshine chuckles as umbrellas collide,
Reminding us all, it's fun to abide.

So let's paint the sky with colors unseen,
With bubbles of laughter, looped in between.
For in every crack, every quirky quirk,
Lies a treasure of joy, in the simple work.

Dreams That Dance Beyond Reason

In the land where socks all misplace,
And cats discuss the human race.
We ask the moon for directions,
While dodging odd reflections.

The toaster sings, the fridge goes boom,
Crumbs create a dance floor in the room.
A parrot starts to play charades,
And time gets lost in silly cascades.

A rollercoaster made from spaghetti,
Zips through our minds, feeling all ready.
Pineapples wear hats, it's quite the sight,
As pancakes flip into the night.

So grab your dreams and let them play,
In a wacky world where we laugh all day.
With giggles and joy, we shun the sane,
In a carnival ride of sweet, funny pain.

Silent Screams in Quiet Rooms

In shadows where thoughts collide and spin,
A sock puppet looks for a way to win.
The clock ticks loud, a hilarious tease,
As we ponder how to fold the cheese.

Whispers of dust bunnies dance with flair,
While the cat plots a grand overtake in the chair.
Tissues tumble, a conspirator's plot,
In the land where giggles tie their knot.

An empty fridge echoes with a sigh,
As we sit and reason, 'Oh my, why?'
With cookies debating their own demise,
In the theatre of dreams, we laugh till we rise.

So shout through silence, let laughter bloom,
In the corners of life, we'll light up the room.
With chuckles and grins, we find our tune,
In the chaos of calm, our hearts are attuned.

Uncharted Territories of the Heart

Where marshmallows float and dreams run wild,
A jellybean prince dances, quite beguiled.
With every heartbeat, a riddle unfurls,
In a land where everyone twirls and swirls.

Maps made of giggles and trails of pie,
The squirrels hold meetings to ask us why.
A compass spun round in a giggly spree,
Leading us boldly to the land of 'wee'.

Love notes scribbled in crayon on walls,
Delivering laughter, the heart gently calls.
While rubber ducks float in a sea of dons,
Writing soft sonnets in uncharted pons.

So leap through the fog with a skip and a hop,
Embracing the joy that won't ever stop.
In the tapestry woven with threads of the sweet,
We find in the chaos, a love complete.

A Symphony of Hidden Truths

In a symphony played by pots and pans,
A dog leads the charge with his marching bands.
With forks that dance and spoons that sing,
Creating a ruckus in everything.

Piano keys play hide-and-seek,
While the blender winks, giving a peek.
A concert of chaos, we cheer and shout,
In this orchestra where laughter's about.

Lost in the notes of a wobbly tune,
With jellybeans serenading the moon.
A chorus of giggles, a cacophony bright,
Where truths hide in marshmallow sparks in the night.

So join the parade of whimsical sounds,
Where reality and laughter know no bounds.
In this silly symphony, our hearts take flight,
Unlocking the secrets hidden in light.

www.ingramcontent.com/pod-product-compliance
Lightning Source LLC
Chambersburg PA
CBHW071852160426
43209CB00003B/528